T0128378

# *Living* To
# Live *Again*

# *Living* To
# Live *Again*

## *Susan R Williams*

WESTBOW
P R E S S®
A DIVISION OF THOMAS NELSON
& ZONDERVAN

WestBow Press books may be ordered through booksellers or by contacting:

WestBow Press
A Division of Thomas Nelson & Zondervan
1663 Liberty Drive
Bloomington, IN 47403
www.westbowpress.com
1 (866) 928-1240

Scripture quotations marked KJV are taken from the King James Version.

ISBN: 978-1-9736-7798-7 (sc)
ISBN: 978-1-9736-7800-7 (hc)
ISBN: 978-1-9736-7799-4 (e)

Library of Congress Control Number: 2019916737

Print information available on the last page.

WestBow Press rev. date: 11/13/2019

# *Dedications*

*In Loving Memory of Odessa Sykes, Arthur L. Sykes,
Herman L Williams, Vivian D. Sykes and Sandra Williams.*

*And to my daughters
E. Brown
Nicole Williams*

*And my grand babies
Love you much!*

# *Foreword*

When you see me put
together,walking with my
head held high and full of
confidence, Never assume I
had an easy life!!
Like they say
"Never Judge a book by it's
cover"

# *Acknowledgments*

I give honor first to the most high God who keeps looking out for me each and everyday. Who saw me before I saw myself. I am truly grateful as well as thankful!

To Mom, Thank you for being you, for instilling the things of God in me from a child. Thanks…

To Nicole Barnes who has been a true friend… thanks for being so supportive on this project.

*F*irst and foremost, I give praise and honor to the Most High God for all he has done for me. Now here it goes—how it all started.

I was born in North Carolina on March 4th to Pearl Sykes who is my mother and my father is Herman Lee Williams. I was raised up with all my siblings. We all grew up together—my sisters and brothers. Some of us weren't born in Connecticut. Some were born in North Carolina. We had a wonderful childhood.

I am the third oldest girl. As a young girl growing up with all my siblings, it was lots of fun. As a child, I was always inquisitive. I often found myself listening to grown-up conversation. That is, I should not have heard them and kept quiet. At that time, I didn't quite understand what was being said, like "you reap what you sow", "if you live long enough, you will understand", and "you don't know until you walk in my shoes". I used to hear this a whole lot. I also witnessed a lot of things that I just couldn't understand as a little girl growing up, but as time continued, I began to understand it.

By and by, my grandmother, whose name was Odessa Sykes, brought us all to Connecticut from North Carolina at an early age. When we first came to Connecticut, my grandmother Odessa and my grandfather Arthur Lee Sykes rented a three-family house. They lived on the first floor, we lived on the third floor, and my uncles lived on the opposite side of the house. All the family lived in this house; I remember it was a big house with a big backyard.

Every day before we went to school, my mother would tell us to hold hands and she would pray for us and tell us to have a good day. Our school was within walking distance of the house, which was nice.

When I was in sixth grade, I signed up for just about everything on the bulletin board—choir, dance, and plays (which I loved). I also brought home an instrument that I couldn't play for anything in this world. It was a violin.

I laugh out loud thinking back now. I think it was the case the violin came in that made me look so distinguished. I thought I knew what I was doing, so I took an interest in trying to play the violin.

I'm laughing out loud as I continue to middle school where I signed up for a lot of activities after school. I loved to run, so I joined the track team where I ran cross country. I always came in first.

I also signed up for captain of cheerleading and rifles at middle school. When I went on to high school, I signed up for cheerleading again. I missed it by a couple of points. I was so disappointed. I knew I should have made the team.

From sixth grade through middle school, I made friends with two girls. We all became the best of friends in a short period of time. I recall one morning walking to school. One of my friends and I looked down on the ground. There was a twenty-dollar bill just waiting for me to pick it up. I saw it first and quickly put my foot on it, then my friend put her foot on it too. We both started laughing. So I did the right thing. I gave her ten dollars and I kept ten dollars. That was fair.

As time continued, I also became friends with another girl. These girls and I built a friendship because we all lived in the same building at the time and we walked to school just about every day. When I attended high school, we all remained friends. I started running track a lot because I loved it, even though some days I was so exhausted from running I would just lay down on the bench in the locker room trying to catch my breath.

So, did I like high school? Yes, but some days were more interesting than others. I had a sister at home who was very sick at the time and my mind was all over the place. But I did love school for the most part.

*N*ow when I talk about high school, our basketball team was awesome. I loved basketball, especially watching the guys who could score. They had a good team and a tight defense. My friends and I tried to attend as many of the games as we possibly could because we had some good-looking guys on the team.

Let me just put it out there in the atmosphere—I wasn't blind. They knew who they were. I just had to say that.

Oh, yeah. I can clearly see now—out of the girls I hung with, the first girl I knew, she knows who she is because her family and my family attended the same church back in the day. So, after and during school sometimes, we would skip one of our classes to hang out with our boyfriends.

I'm shaking my head at this. I can tell you now. I am really laughing hard about this.

Now, if I say I got your back, you can bank on it. I was her alibi and she was mine. And when I was questioned about her whereabouts, I said I didn't know anything about anything. I'm still laughing because true friends are rare, and I wasn't going to tell. I'm laughing out loud again.

While at school, these are the classes that I loved: Gym, cooking, science, and English. So, after school, my friend and

I would go to the girls' club where we were taught how to cook and make pigs in a blanket—which I hate to this very day—and pizza cups. Our teacher at the girls' club also showed us how to make clothes—skirts and jumpsuits. It was so much fun! I'm shaking my head once again about that poor jumpsuit I needed assistance with.

We mingled with other girls that we knew. I liked the girls' club. One day we were asked by one of the teachers to write an essay about the girls' club. For some reason, she singled me out. I do remember writing the essay about the girls' club. I received an award for it at a dinner. That took me by surprise. I had no idea that my essay would win! I was so ecstatic.

Now, shift gears. As time went on, my father would come to visit us sometimes. He would leave and come back from North Carolina to Connecticut to stay with us for a long period of time, and I loved that. I loved having him around because he made me laugh. He loved the outdoors. He would always keep busy. He would go in the backyard and plant carrots, collard greens, tomatoes, squash, okra, and cucumbers. He would take the grapes off the vines and make wine out of them. It was something to see! Then he would go to the store and buy two big garbage pails to preserve the wine. I was always curious about how it turned out.

I remember my sister and I tasting the wine. We were teenagers at the time. After my father went into the house to check on dinner, my sister and I tasted the wine. When my mother called us for dinner, we were feeling kind of tipsy.

Oh, yeah. We couldn't sit at the dinner table. That is when my father got up from the dinner table, opened the back door, and noticed that the lid of the garbage pail of wine was slightly tilted, and knew we had been drinking some of his wine. We had stuck our heads down in the big pail that was filled to the brim. This was homemade grape wine. I recall my sister and I—all we did was laugh. I do not remember getting in trouble. I do remember my mother saying that we were drinking.

I also recall those country meals my father would prepare. One of my favorites was chicken and dumplings and homemade blueberry pie. Oh, boy. It was so delicious. My father could really cook.

I also remember that some of our childhood friends who lived next door came over just about every day after school. We would sit around telling jokes and playing games. The jokes we told were so hilarious. I would just fall to the ground due to laughing so hard, holding my stomach.

Just sitting on the front porch, my siblings and I watched cars go by, naming and claiming them by saying "that's my car". My siblings and I would play hopscotch, Double Dutch, Mother may I, and hide-and-go-seek. Being that there were seven of us, we needed no additional company because we had each other's backs. I always want to keep those memories alive.

I also remember my cousins who lived right across the street. They had a very big black dog who they called Smoky. Oh, boy! Here we go. He used to chase us up and down the stairs. Just about every time we played outside, he was not disciplined, so he would come outside barking, looking to terrorize us. He got on my last nerve. We would all take off running. One day, the dog bit my brother's leg. Thank God it wasn't serious.

We had lots of friends who lived in the neighborhood, as well as lots of fun kids who came over and hung out. I remember a boatyard across the street where the owner used to sell hamburgers, fries, and hot dogs with chili which were out of this world. What a nice street to live on. We would go over to the boatyard to look at the boats out in the water and make conversation with the owners. Then later we would go play in our big backyard where we would pull up carrots from the garden, then go in the house and wash them off to eat them.

We also used to take my mother's pots, pans, spoons, and forks outside to the backyard to dig up dirt and make mud pies. Then we would pull off the leaves from the trees and make believe they were collard greens and cut them up. Then we would take my mother's dish detergent, a bowl, and a fork, pour water in the bowl and beat it up until we saw sludge. Then we pretended we were making icing for a cake.

We did all of this while my mother was at work, but we knew when we got through playing with these items we had to put them all back before our mother came home from work. We had so much fun. This was our secret. Back then, we never said anything about that because we all would have gotten reprimanded. My mother did not believe in timeouts. If we did something wrong, we would get a spanking.

She worked at a daycare taking care of babies, and when my mother couldn't work anymore, she was never too prideful to ask for assistance. My mother made sure we had plenty of food. She would go grocery shopping when my brother, the baby of the family, was about two or three years old at the time, I believe. One night when everyone was asleep, he went up the stairs and reached on top of the fridge to help himself to whatever he could get. He opened a can of soda, a bag of cookies, and a bag of chips. He left a trail of evidence, and the next morning my mother noticed the cookie trail and the opened can of soda on the steps.

My mother thought it was one of the older kids, but not so! It was that baby boy who was eating up all the snacks! I laugh out loud remembering. How he opened that can of soda it is a mystery until this very day. Only—and I mean only—God knows how he did it. So, Baby Boy kind of got us all in trouble because my mother didn't believe her baby boy did such a thing. But he did!

Now the two twins of the family used to sing this song every time they woke up and I don't know where they got it from because I never heard it before. They were on the beat with it too. It went, "Now I am woke, Daddy. Now I am woke, Daddy," repeatedly. They were standing up in their crib in their pajamas, side by side, rocking back and forth. My father would hear them and immediately come upstairs, change their diapers, and run downstairs to the kitchen to prepare two bottles of milk. He brought it to them, laid both down in their crib, and they were quiet after that.

*M*y mother worked hard at keeping us all in check and in order. She brought all of us up in the church. We went to church as a family. Can I get an Amen, readers? I know a lot of you have heard this thing my mother said, "As long as you live in my house and under my roof, you are going to church."

You see, back in those days there were lots of church revivals going on, also a lot of miracles happening all around us. As I recall, my mother instilled the belief of God in us as little babies. We were taught a lot of things in Sunday school.

I remember my siblings and I playing outside with some friends. My mother would call us all in the house. We knew the drill—it was time to get ready for church. We knew exactly what time it was even on school nights. Some of our friends we played with would laugh and say, "Y'all go to church a lot!" In the back of my mind, I use to say, *I am tired of going.* It seemed like we had to go to church just about every night, regardless if we had school the next day or not.

There were no excuses but to get on the bus. The driver was so persistent. If he said seven in the evening, that was it. It was, he stated, because he had other people to pick up.

I remember my mother on Saturday nights. She would put out everybody's clothes, so we knew exactly what we were wearing. There was no getting up in the morning and rumbling around acting like you didn't know what you were going to wear. My mother was already ahead of the game, so don't you try to play. The girls' and boys' clothes were laid out down to our socks and shoes.

For all seven of us, my mother always bought us nice things to wear. If she bought for one, she would buy for all. There was no favoritism. And when we arrived at church she would put us all in the front row because she sang in the choir, and that way she could keep a close eye on us.

She loved children. It was obvious. She had seven! I remember my mother's sisters coming over. They used to go out shopping a lot and my mother would always leave my oldest sister in charge. She would make sure we ate all our vegetables. She would prepare dinner for us, and after dinner, there was a chore list on the refrigerator with our names on it that we had to follow. When my father was around, he would cook some of those down south, mouthwatering meals that would make you kick off your shoes and say, "Hey, fix me a plate. I am staying for dinner!"

I remember this one time, something broke in the house while we were playing. My father stood up for me by saying, "It wasn't Susie. Some of the other children did it."

My mother would always keep gospel music playing throughout the house.

Vivian—whom my grandmother and grandfather raised—she was a great sister, very humble and sweet. I remember one night we were all in the house playing. We saw someone we didn't quite recognize standing on our front porch. We locked the front door and ran out the backdoor, straight over the bridge to my grandmother's house. At that time, my grandmother lived right around the corner. We didn't live that far from her. When we reached her house, we were all out of breath. She asked us what happened. We told her the story, and then she said, "Stay here until your mother gets home." That was fine with us.

Readers, back in the day we used to call our mother by her name, Pearl, instead of Mama. Until one day, this lady who went to the same church we attended came over to my aunt and uncle's house who lived around the corner. She said if we would stop calling our mother "Pearl" and start calling her "Mama" she would treat all seven of us. So, we said okay and she did just that. Ever since that day, we called our mother "Mama".

*S*peaking of my mother, she is a strong woman—a woman of character and integrity. She was a good provider and was very strict. She always made sure we didn't go without. We had more than enough for a mother who had seven kids. God blessed us a thousand times over. Thank God for blessing us with a roof over our heads, food on our table, clothes on our backs, and shoes on our feet. To God be all the praise and glory for keeping us together.

Mother made sure everything was together. She always kept a clean house and she raised us up to be clean kids. She didn't allow clutter in corners or dust or dirty dishes in her sink. Her two best cleaning products she uses to this very day. Everything was in order.

We were taught that you must be kind and loving toward others. We were taught the right way to go. We were brought up the right way, with good morals and respect for others. Before went to bed each night, we had to take a bath.

My mother didn't like a messy house. She made sure we had assigned chores which my oldest sister supervised, making sure it was done every Friday evening. And when we finished, she would check behind us to see if it was done properly.

My mother made sure we had a hot breakfast every

morning and prepared our lunches for school every night. I watched her. We also had a nice healthy dinner every night.

We all stayed together. We couldn't spend the night at anyone's house— family only, so don't even ask.

The holidays were an amazing time of year. For Thanksgiving and Christmas, my mother would cook all kinds of stuff. I remember a lot of my mother's recipes to this very day, like chopped barbecue (hallelujah). She used to say, "If you watch me, one day you will know how to cook." Most of the women who were born and raised in North Carolina knew how to cook, and if they didn't, they weren't watching.

Before Christmas, she would also tell us to write down what we wanted. She planned ahead of time, so we could have what we asked for. The night before Christmas, she would make us big Christmas bags filled with lots of fruits, nuts, and candy. This was tradition. This is something my grandmother used to do for her family back in the day, so my mother picked up the tradition and did this every Christmas for her family until we got up in age. We used to have so many gifts. There was no room left to put the gifts. We had to stack them on top of each other, and when family and friends came over, they were astonished by what they saw.

*I* have so many wonderful memories until this very day about the holidays. Christmas is, and shall always be, my favorite time of the year. We always took lots of pictures. My father spent lots of holidays with us. He would come and go. He would come up from North Carolina on the bus and stay with us for months. Even when my mother and father separated, my father was very much involved in our lives.

I also recall my mother used to take all seven of us down south to see our father. Just about every summer on the bus, I remember the fried chicken sandwiches, bologna and cheese sandwiches, ham and cheese sandwiches, and peanut butter and jelly sandwiches. We had all kinds of snacks to eat along the way.

When my father wasn't around, my mother held it down like a woman is supposed to, and that is real, real talk. I have seen her be both parents. She set an example for her family. She never had men running in and out of her house. She never had men around her girls, because even though she was a Christian woman, she said, "I don't want to have to hurt somebody if they mess with us." Mainly, she meant the girls. It was five girls and two boys. She didn't play. She would let any man know that she was a married woman, and she took her vows seriously—regardless of whether my father was absent or present—and she didn't have time for their foolishness.

One day, this man was trying to come on to my mother. She basically set him straight nicely. Boy did I laugh. She set the standard—and I mean a high standard.

I am very proud of my mother. I must say that because I never saw her with another man, only my father. It's the life she lived before her children. I truly thank God for the life she lived around us.

When my mother was in school back in the day, she would protect herself. She had lots of brothers and wasn't scared because she learned how to fight and defend herself. She beat the boys up—and the girls, as well. If they bothered her, she would let them know straight up, "I am not the one laughing out loud."

I have seen my mother through the years suffer with asthma. Some days were worse than others. This went on for months and years—in and out of the hospital. At the hospital, code 99 was called twice or more. I used to always pray to God to let my mother be okay, and I can say this now—she has overcome it. To God be all the glory.

My sisters, Vivian and two of my other siblings, also used to suffer tremendously from asthma. I used to watch. But my oldest sister, Vivian, who also suffered for months and years with this baffling disease, was taken from this life in August of 1981.

*I*t was a hot summer day. I will never forget it as long as I live. I remember coming home in the afternoon from school. At the time, we lived in a high-rise building. As I approached the building, I looked up to see my sister, Vivian, looking out the window. When I saw her, she had on a lavender robe. She was bending over, looking down. I rushed up the stairs. The elevator was not working at the time. When I got to the door, I rang the bell because I didn't have my key. My mother answered. She was talking to my aunt who was visiting with us at the time.

When I got inside, I went straight to my sister's room. I said, "Vivian, what is wrong?" She couldn't talk to me because she could barely breathe, and that scared me so badly. That is when I started panicking. Anxiety had shown up. I told my sister to quickly call the ambulance. I remember Vivian having tears in her eyes as I called out to my mother. I said, "Vivian has to go to the hospital, like, right now!"

My sister, Sandra, came running. She had called the ambulance many times. They kept saying they were on the way, so Sandra let my mother know that the ambulance was aware. That was when my mother and my aunt came into my sister's bedroom. They both took one of her arms and slowly started to walk her out of the bedroom. Vivian's breathing got heavier and heavier as she approached the front door of our apartment. I heard her say, "Oh!" as she bent over, holding her stomach as they proceeded to the hallway. Vivian collapsed right before our eyes.

I didn't know what to do. I was so nervous and scared as I looked down at her. She wasn't moving at all. I remember a neighbor coming out of her apartment. She had a blanket in her hand and put it on my sister to keep her warm. That is when Sandra and I ran downstairs to see where the ambulance was and what was taking them so long. We were both hysterical and in panic mode.

As we waited downstairs, the ambulance took forever to arrive. Time had gone by, and when they *did* come, they had to take the stairs because the elevator wasn't in working order. At the time, I couldn't believe what was going on. My sister and I were going up and down, checking on Vivian.

I saw water passing from my sister as she laid in front of our door. I remember my aunt saying, "She has a pulse." My aunt seemed to know a lot because she worked at the hospital, so that was a good sign that my aunt knew exactly what was happening.

Finally, thank God, the paramedics showed up with oxygen tanks. I also remember a neighbor came out trying to lend a helping hand for my sister. What a big help! Meanwhile, paramedics put the oxygen mask on my sister and did a couple of other procedures before they moved her. Vivian was not hyperventilating. She remained calm, breathing rapidly trying to catch her breath. "God," I prayed, "Help us today!"

Then they proceeded to slowly carry her down the flight of stairs on a stretcher. It was kind of difficult for the paramedics to do their job since the elevator was broken. Oh, what a day! People were standing outside just looking and asking questions. All I kept hearing were people saying, "What happened? What happened?"

I was in a state of shock as people stood by looking on. Friends wanted to know if she was going to be alright. I kept the faith by saying yes. I remember also saying to friends that my sister had an asthma attack. I kept telling myself that she was going to be all right.

The ambulance took her to the hospital. My aunt and mother both got in the car and went to the hospital. My sister went into the house and I stayed outside talking to my acquaintances and friends, hoping to hear some good news.

Soon, enough time had passed that it started to get dark. All of a sudden, I looked up. My aunts, mother, and cousin drove up. Everyone got out of the car. I couldn't understand why everybody was in one car.

I looked at their faces. They looked sad. I said, "How is Vivian doing?" I asked the question a couple of times. My mother said, "Come upstairs. We are going to talk about it." I kept on being impatient, wanting to know right now what was going on with my sister. That is when my cousin said to me, "Vivian died."

Oh, no. I just took off running down the street like a madwoman as fast as I could, not looking back. I recall this guy who lived in the same building trying to catch me and calm me down. I don't know how he calmed me down. I was a mess. I wanted to die, readers, on that day.

I will repeat—I literally wanted to die that particular day. I am not just saying this. I didn't want to live at all. I was looking for a car, bus, truck, train—*anything* to come by and just hit me, run me over, to just kill me and put me out of my misery. That is how I felt in my spirit, but for some reason, there was nothing coming in my direction.

**D**arkness had shown its face. I felt like time had stopped. I believe I would have jumped out in front of whatever was moving that day, and I know my soul would have been in torment. I couldn't believe it or receive it. This was unbelievable, shocking news that made me drop. I couldn't process it in my head. It was not registering at all. It made no sense. How could this be? My sister, she was so young. I wanted somebody to help me understand the word "dead". I was bewildered. I was devastated and confused, as well as perplexed. What a tearful day.

Even as I write this book, I must pause for a minute. As I reflect back, tears begin to form in my eyes. This was a tragic and unexpected death. Suddenly, so many things were going on with me. I was all over the place. I just wanted the pain to stop. Was there anything to take away the pain that was in my heart? "Not my sister. Not my sister," I kept saying. I said to God, "You should have taken me! I am the bad sister! How are my mother and father going to get through this?"

I knew my mother was a strong woman. I knew she was a Christian woman who believed in God strongly, but this was hard. There is no pill for the kind of pain we were all feeling. This was death that I am talking about. How do you process death? Somebody tell me, please! Tell me. How do you process never seeing your loved ones again?

*M*e, my sisters, and brothers were very close. Vivian is dead. I couldn't receive that in my head for anything. It didn't even sound right. It was like a numbness came over me. People always say you have one life to live. I knew that, but at the time I didn't want the life that I had been given. I wanted that hurt to go away so badly. I couldn't talk to her again or see her. I didn't believe it, and I assure you, none of my family did either—not at all. One minute she was here, the next she was gone.

Here my mother was planning a funeral. I recall the night of the wake, my aunt kept asking my uncle to go into the funeral home to see if it was really her. We were all standing outside the funeral home, sad. My uncle went in to make sure it was her. He came out and told my aunt, "It's her."

I was praying—I was hoping it wasn't true. That is when my aunt became weak and so did I. We were in denial for a long time. I am the type of person where I really don't believe anything until you show me or prove it to me. Sorry. This is me I am talking about until I saw her lying in that casket. She was a good sister.

The day of the funeral, our pastor preached at the funeral. Lots of family from out of town attended the funeral home service. Also, lots of friends who really liked my sister attended. I remember walking up to the casket. I looked down at my sister. It was Vivian, but it still didn't register in my head. I looked around, saw some of my family members crying. My aunts and uncles, how they loved her. She used to babysit for one of my aunts. She would watch my cousin when he was a little boy. She wouldn't let him get dirty for anything. She had powder everywhere to make sure he stayed cool because it was a very hot summer day. She would come home from work, go outside and talk to her best friend.

*I* recall the day my sister died—August 1981—due to an asthma attack that snatched her life from her. Some of our friends were giving a party that night. They canceled the party due to my sister's death. This was heartbreaking news.

Prior to my sister dying, I can remember one night. It was a lot of us. We went to the beach. We all took off our shoes. We held hands and went into the water—just our feet. I remember Vivian saying, "This summer will not be the same." I heard her say that but didn't really take it seriously at the time. So, I said, "What do you mean?" Then her best friend said, "Yeah, what does that mean?" Then she said, "You will see." It sounded so strange, but she had a very serious look on her face. I kept pondering it in my head.

I always admired Vivian's style. I wanted to hang out with my sister and her friends, but I wasn't in their age bracket, so I used to just hang around them outside the building to hear what their conversations were about. They would be dressed up, just standing outside the building looking very nice. I really liked that about my sister—how she kept herself together—she definitely had style. When she came in from work, she and her best friend would talk on the phone and then they would go outside together. Her friend lived in the same building.

Oh, how she loved her sling-back shoes. She had them in every color. And how she loved the color lavender.

She used to do her own hair so nice. She also grew her own nails out so long. When they used to break, she would put them in a box, and I would get some of them and glue them on my own nails when she wasn't looking.

She used to hang out at her friend's house, and they would play all kinds of music. It used to be a couple of them harmonizing, hitting those notes, singing songs—and they could really sing. I will give them their props.

As time went on, a sad day had approached. There was no sunshine on that day, and even if there was, I couldn't see it. It was a dark day, but every day looked dark to me. The day my sister died, this was something we had to endure at the time. I kept repeating, "God, why did you take my sister? You should have taken me!"

I was hurting. I was in a state of shock like everyone else. What a dark day for my family, a very devastating time. It was heartrending, very sad. We were grieving for a long time. Vivian was only twenty years old. She had not begun to live her life. She was engaged to this wonderful guy and did not get a chance to get married. He was in the army at the time. He used to write to my sister all the time. I used to read some of the letters he sent. I was always in her stuff when she wasn't watching.

This guy had plans. He truly loved my sister and I knew it. I remember when he came home from the army. He came to see my sister, and they looked so good together. I used to hear my sister talking to her best friend about moving out of town. I guess they were making future plans. They talked about moving one day, but that one day never came. It was so sad.

*A*s time went on, our family was able to cope and come to grips with my oldest sister's death because we knew she was sick for a while with this asthma. The good news was she was saved, so that was a good thing. We had lots of family, friends, and neighbors, as well as a church family for moral support standing by our side through this time of sorrow and grief. Some people would give their sympathy, saying that everything was going to be fine, this too shall pass. I said, "I will hopefully see her again one day on the other side. This is my prayer."

Then another death occurred. Again, this was an extremely overwhelming and distressing time for my family, as well as painful, tragic, and upsetting for all of us. On April 1, 1984, my sister Sandra died. She was diagnosed with this baffling disease called cancer. She had cancer of the liver. It showed its ugly face. I watched this terminal illness take a toll on my sister. Her whole demeanor and attitude started to change. Some days she was in good spirits, and then other days not so good. I understood because she was sick. I said to myself, *What on earth is going on?*

She was in and out of the hospital for treatment. The nurses used to come in and out of her room. Some days she would tell them, "I am not giving out any more blood today!" She got to the point where she didn't want them to keep sticking her with needles. Sometimes she would get frustrated when the nurse came into her room. She would push the button on the side of the bed and make the bed go way up to the ceiling, as high as it would go until it couldn't go any further. I would laugh. My sister was only nineteen years old. Her life had not even begun. But she definitely had a sense of humor and that made me laugh.

She was strong. I remember a nurse came to the house to take care of her. My other sister used to assist the nurse, too. My mother's cousin who was originally from North Carolina used to come up and visit her family then come over and stay with us. She would pray for my sister and rub her down. She always had her bible open to a scripture. I recall her saying, "You don't have to read the whole bible. Just get one scripture and place it in your spirit." She comforted my sister. She was a big help to our family as well.

I also remember a family that came to help. I'd never seen anything like it. I believe to this very day that they were angels who were on an assignment to help our family through this experience. They showed so much love, compassion, and affection. They were heaven-sent. I remember them coming to the house, sitting down, getting to know each and every one of us by name. They asked us what we liked and disliked—just making conversation—and on the weekdays, they would bring food by, already prepared. I also remember how kind and loving these people were because on Christmas Eve they took all of us to a church. It was such a nice church and that is not all they did. They brought all seven of us including my mother gifts for Christmas—things that we had told them that we liked.

I remember receiving a watch. I actually have a picture of it because I was the one in the family who loved to take pictures. I used to say to my mother, "If you don't have any pictures, you don't have any memories." Some of you may disagree. It's my opinion. No problem. So, I made sure I had plenty of pictures so I could look back and reminisce one day about the good times we all shared together.

I remember one morning, I was in the room with my sister. She was lying in bed. I walked in and she said, "Come here."

I didn't know what she wanted so I came closer to her. She said, "You are pregnant." She said it a couple of times.

I said, "What did you say?"

She repeated it.

I tried to deny it. She said, "I know because of your pulse up under your neck."

I said, "I hope you don't tell mother until I get a chance to."

She assured me that she wouldn't. So I basically did whatever she asked of me, so she wouldn't tell my mother before I had a chance to do so.

During that time, my father was in town from North Carolina. I don't remember how I told my mother and father that I was pregnant. I remember when my oldest daughter was born, my sister tried to hold her. She said she was going to be a mean baby, so she gave me money to buy her a baby bag. I did just that.

Sandra loved football and basketball. She was a tomboy. She loved her jeans with a fresh white t-shirt and sneakers—name brand, of course. She loved to iron her shoestrings and wear her hair in an afro. She loved to put a net on her hair so it would look neat. The guys were crazy about her because she could play the game just as well as they could. Most of the guys were shocked. She loved to play sports. She loved to run track, as well. She was on a girls' basketball team in middle school, and with her being on the team they never lost. I used to watch her play and used to be in the bleachers cheering her on, letting her teammates know, "That's my sister! That's my sister!" because she was the star of the team.

I never saw a girl play basketball like that, especially hitting those three-pointers. Wow and wow. I heard the crowd go "ooh". I was so amazed and proud and glad she was my sister. I didn't know she had game like that. Wow. They even had shirts made up when she went on to play baseball with the Devastators. When she played baseball, her coach loved her.

I remember her running with these girls. She took off like a plane leaving them in the dust. I also remember my sister playing football outside. The guys would say, "I want Sandra on my team!" Then after a while, the guys would say, "Where are you going?" She used to tell her friends, "I am getting ready to go to church." They would try to convince her to stay and play some more, but they already knew she was going to church. She really loved church.

Also, there was a church van that would pick all seven of us up, including my mother who would be the last to get in the van. She made sure nobody was left behind. My sister held her bible in her hand every time she went to church. She was saved long before my sister asked the question because she and my oldest sister Vivian had a conversation about salvation. She told her this one day, "If you aren't saved, you'd better get saved."

As time went by, as I said earlier, she was diagnosed with cancer of the liver. My mother was told by the doctors that she could have had a liver transplant, but my sister refused, and no one could persuade her otherwise. I remember her eyes turning yellow and her features starting to change. Her hair didn't fall out, but it was thin, very soft, and easy to manage.

What she loved was for someone to give her a massage. She didn't care who you were, as long as you had two hands and they were usable. She used to make whoever came over to our house to visit give her a massage because you weren't going to stand around looking in her face. She would say, "What are you looking at?" And boy, did I laugh for hours.

Some of those who I am talking about were my cousins, which I have a lot of. They had to massage her. She would give some of them a couple of dollars, and some of them she wouldn't. Some of my cousins felt sorry for her. I could see it in their faces because I knew they just did it out of generosity. They felt sympathy for her because she was sick, and they didn't want to make her sad. Their hands were getting so tired as I looked on, laughing out loud. But my sister didn't want to hear that. She was in command and in control. They knew it. Who was going to tell her no? And if you did, you just found a replacement—do a shift change or something. Who is up next? State your name and make sure your hands are working and then you may take a break.

Sometimes she would tell them, "I am not your friend." She would be one of my cousin's friends that day, and then she would tell my other cousin, "I am not your friend today." She had jokes. I used to just laugh because it was funny to me.

My aunt also used to come over a lot, and for some reason, she used to pin her up in a corner and repeatedly say, "What are you going to do? What are you going to do?" This was before she was really sick. My aunt used to play along with her and start laughing. Sandra loved my aunt.

I recall one day, I was getting ready to go to school. This was my senior year and I needed extra points to graduate. My sister kept on saying, "Don't go to school today. Stay here with me." And when she said that, my eyes filled with tears because we shared the same room at the time. I used to look at her and feel so sorry for her. Tears would come and I held them back because I didn't want her to see me cry. Sometimes during the night, I used to look over at her to see if she was okay. Sometimes she would be awake and ask me to get her something to drink, and I would do just that. Then she would ask me to massage her arm and some days I would stay home with her.

Just about every day, my sister didn't want me to go to school, and the days I did go, I wasn't focused on school. My mind was on my sister. I couldn't function the way I wanted to. As time went by, I didn't get the chance to walk with my class. It didn't bother me because the time I spent with my sister was worth it. If I had to do it over, I would because I valued the time I shared with my sister. You cannot get time back. Would have, could have, should have, but I still received my high school diploma, readers. I still walked with my cap and gown. What a wonderful feeling! To God be the glory.

There was a social worker who would come by and take Sandra out to lunch and do things with her. I would stay home with her and go out to lunch because she asked me to. I wanted to be there for my sister no matter what. She was well taken care of. She had a lot of love and support from family and friends—those who she wanted to bother with, and those who she didn't.

My father was very close to my sister. How he loved her, so he waited on her hand and foot. He used to fix her whatever she wanted. She loved chicken gizzards with her hot sauce. That was one of her favorites.

I remember one Sunday, my mother went off to church. That Sunday, I didn't go. I wanted to stay with my sister. My uncle was at the house lying on the couch, and my other sister was home at the time too. My father was also there on that day. My sister was in a lot of pain—excruciating pain. She began repeatedly shouting at the capacity of her voice, "I am tired! I am tired! I am tired!" I witnessed the pain she went through. My sister endured pain on that day and I couldn't help her. That's when I knew she was giving up.

*S* unday, April 1, 1984, the ambulance was called once again. My uncle called the church to tell my mother what was going on. My father went with Sandra to the hospital. My mother and her sisters all went to the hospital from church. When we called to check on my sister, all we kept hearing was that the nurses were making her comfortable, and we all knew exactly what would come next because we had been through it before. But we always wished for the best news. So, I stayed at home with my daughter, waiting to hear good news.

I remember it seemed like the longest day and longest night. Suddenly, the doorbell rang. I couldn't understand why nobody used their key that evening. My father came in crying. My mother was walking slowly behind him, as well as some other family members. My mother said, "Sandra died."

All I remember was screaming at the top of my voice. I remember jumping up and down. I laid on the floor crying. A very close friend of mine who lived upstairs came down to be with me in this time of sorrow. What a dark Sunday evening that had arrived at our door. It felt like nothing was moving. All I could hear was sobbing. I never heard my father cry until that dreadful, dreadful day.

My sister died. How she loved my father. They were

very close. He did whatever she asked him to do. He would prepare lots of meals for her and go to the store for her without complaining as many times as she wanted.

I could not process this once again, trying to understand this in my head. I was in a state of shock again, but I knew she was too sick as I looked at her day in and day out. She was a fighter. She held on as long as she could. But I knew eventually she would get tired. She couldn't live like that, no matter how bad I wanted her to stay.

I remember my daughter's father kept trying to calm me down. My mother said my father was with her in the hospital room when she died. My father broke down. It ripped him apart. He kept on saying, "She is gone! She is gone!" And I couldn't understand what and why this happened again to our family.

My mother raised all of us in the church. We were a very close family—not perfect, though. Now, here we were preparing for my second sister's funeral. The day of the funeral, our pastor, he preached to those gathered. I walked up to the casket. She was dressed in all white. She looked very peaceful. Her face glowed. Then I said quietly, "I will see you again." There was a nice poem about my sister that a member of the church read about how she loved football.

I loved my sister, and I told her often. I just wanted answers. The grief I felt… "Why, God? Why?"

I know, readers.

You should never question God, but I did.

Someone asked me, "Did you cuss God out after the loss of your sisters?" I told them I would never do such a thing to God because He is my lifeline.

But I couldn't understand, because back in the day, I used to see miracles right in the church. As a young girl growing up in the church, I saw miracles right before my very eyes, and it was not a myth. I witnessed all these miracles for real. I was astonished by it. People who couldn't speak now talked, people who were in wheelchairs who had not walked in years got up and started walking. People on crutches threw them away and began to run around the church. They stood up straight and walked around. The deaf began to hear, and then they began to praise God. I witnessed a lot of things.

Let me remind you, I was a young girl at the time. Seeing all of this, it frightened me to my core when I witnessed certain things. We were told to hold our bibles when certain things occurred.

*T*he church that I attended, we used to go to a lot of church revivals. I had seen a lot of miracles at a very young age. I was looking for a miracle only because I witnessed and saw so many miracles back in the day. I was looking for someone with the power of God in their life to bring both of my sisters back. Nobody had the power to save either one of my sisters—if they did, I didn't know who they were.

Going to church was all we knew from babies. It was embedded in us early on. My parents raised us in the church, and now we had to face this again—death. Sometimes I would wonder if I was next because it just seemed like that to me. Was this my reality? Because I was the third oldest girl, and the two oldest were gone. I felt this in my subconscious. Could this be true, or was it all in my mind? Could it be?

I knew my mother was a strong woman. My father—I saw tears running down his face when Vivian died. Two daughters gone so close to one another. Who could endure such pain? I couldn't even imagine how my parents were feeling and how they contained it all back to back. The two oldest, nineteen and twenty years old. "God," I prayed. "Please help us."

My mother said if she didn't know God at the time—and these are her own words that came out of her mouth—she said, "I would have ended up probably in the crazy house if it had not been for God."

I used to watch her closely to see when she was going to break down, and I knew God was with her, as well as with us all. I knew my sisters were sick. I thought she would be okay. This was sudden death. Unexpected. But I also knew she was sick and tired, and she couldn't live in that kind of pain for long. I saw her on that dreadful and dark day, readers. Most of you have experienced death. This was one of the hardest things I have ever dealt with in my life. Not one sister, but two.

It was so hard for me to internalize that both of my sisters were gone. This hurt, because you see, after the death of my sisters, I didn't care about going to church. I wanted to escape. I didn't want to hear about church or anything about it. I wanted to run away from everything and everyone, even the pain of this tragic situation. But I knew that running away could not bring my two sisters back because the pain was with me wherever I went.

I felt like God didn't love me or care. Why did he let this happen to us twice? I was lost. People used to come over asking us, "Are you okay? How do you feel?"

No. We weren't okay. That was the *dumbest* question you could ever ask anyone in their time of sorrow. I was very angry. I will say it again; I was very angry, mad, irritated, and frustrated. All the above and whatever came after that, all in the same breath—mad at people and God. At the time, I just wanted my two oldest sisters to come back. There were some

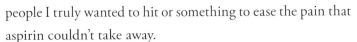

people I truly wanted to hit or something to ease the pain that aspirin couldn't take away.

Someone said, "Oh, it's going to be alright." I wanted to know when it would be alright. Could you give me a specific date or time?

"Oh, they went to a better place."

I wanted to say to them, "If you don't get away from me, you are going somewhere too." But my mother always said you must respect your elders."

It's just something about death. I know, readers. Some of you can relate to what I am saying. It made me angry—very angry and mad. The more I thought about it, the angrier I was. I was very hateful. I had a bad attitude. If you said anything to me, I would snap you up. I carried that around in me for years. I was looking to slap anyone who said anything stupid to me. I always thought that you should think before you open your mouth, and if you can't help the situation, then don't hurt anyone. Just be quiet.

These are my feelings. This is what I felt at that time. I couldn't comprehend the loss of my sisters. I started to question my existence. It was a very difficult time for me psychologically. There was pain—emotional pain. I wasn't grasping the situation mentally, to the point where I didn't feel anything. I felt like a zombie, dead to the extreme and wanting to die myself, but I couldn't die.

Yes, I will reiterate—I literally wanted to die after the death of my two sisters. Things were not the same at all. I started hanging out with people in bad places where I had no business being. I felt like life had dealt me a bad card, and readers, I am not afraid to tell you this. I was getting high, started smoking marijuana, and that led to another substance that was introduced to me that I started indulging in later down the road.

*I* was trying to stop the pain in my heart. I was dealing with the death of my sisters in a different way. I couldn't cope with their deaths. It would play in my head over and over and over again to the point where I wanted to join them. I truly didn't think anybody cared about me. I didn't have anyone I could talk to or confide in who I looked up to but my grandmother. I wasn't going to tell her what I was doing and what I was dealing with. But you see, after you lose someone so dear to you, a piece of you is missing, and that's what happened to me. I was missing, and the only person who could bring me back to me was God.

Listen, readers, hear me and hear me good because sometimes we find things to make us feel good for that moment. You know what your feel-good is in your time of sorrow over a person or a thing.

I am not talking to everybody because some are stronger than others. Some make it back, and some don't. Well, I can confess that was one of my weak points when I indulged in something that I shouldn't have indulged in. I am here to tell you it wasn't the cure. I felt worse and worse. You see, you can numb the pain for a while, but eventually it will wear off, and then you find yourself back at it again.

I knew I had to face my conscience the next day. I used to hang out on those streets, so I know what I know. You see, people said, "Oh, I am here for you!" and somewhere down the line, I never saw that person again until the next funeral or wedding. And that is factual when it comes to me. So, I started hanging out and skipping out. While hanging out I met this guy who kept coming around, telling me that he liked me. That was nice at the time.

He was running a game, telling me all kinds of things to get my attention. Now, readers, it doesn't stop here. There's more to this story. I was young—a teenager at the time. There is a saying, "Young, dumb, and out of control." I liked the nightlife. I used to drink and go club-hopping just about every night looking for a good time and looking for love that I thought I could find. I didn't know my purpose at all and had no meaning in life, but it wasn't what it appeared to be, hanging out in those clubs. I would dress up all the time. This is what made me happy. Even if I felt sad, I would dress up. I would put on a nice outfit, my high-heeled shoes, put my makeup on—and guess what? You couldn't tell me I didn't look good at the time.

But hear this: You can look good but not feel good. That was me. I was messed up emotionally from the hurts of my past, from things I carried deep within, my heart so broken. But who could see the cracks as time went on?

*Y*ears later, something happened again, and just when you think you are getting on with your life, starting to feel a little bit better and see the sun again, something else occurs.

So, as time went on, my father, who I truly loved, was diagnosed with this deadly, baffling disease called cancer of the bone. He hid it from us very well. We were informed that my father went to the doctor and that is what they discovered when we went to visit him in North Carolina. He was in good spirits, just walking around doing what he normally did. The cancer had not yet taken effect on him. He would always say, "Y'all made it!" and we would say, "Yes!" when we visited him in the nursing facility. He was fine. He let us know that he would be going home soon. He appeared to be fine—no pain. My mother would always pray for him. We would be sitting in the visiting area, just laughing.

My mother and father, they had separated but they never got a divorce. They truly loved each other. They had their ups and downs, but they always came together and talked it out. My mother had seven children by one man.

My father did not like Connecticut. My mother didn't have a problem with it. He liked North Carolina. He was a landscaper. He loved his garden. People used to stop and ask him, "How did you do that?" and ask him to come over to their houses to landscape and they would pay him. He was a handyman. He loved his flowers and garden.

He also collected antiques, and at Christmas people used to stop by. Cars lined up by his house to see his decorations. He had lights that came from the east, west, north, and south—up from everywhere. Lights came up from the ground and wrapped all around the house, totaling over a thousand lights or so. Mr. Claus and Mrs. Claus stood on the rooftop with the reindeer. It was something to see.

My father was an extraordinary person. He could fix anything broken. He was very creative with his hands. He kept his house clean, didn't want anyone to mess with his things, and made that known. He loved anything to do with the outdoors. He loved his animals—cats, dogs, pigs, horses, roosters, and so on.

I remember one of his roosters pecked me in the face when I was a little girl sucking my finger. My grandmother—his mother—came running out of the house with her gun. She killed the wrong rooster.

My father told me this story. I remember a news reporter came to my father's house to interview him. They asked my father a lot of questions about his life. I remember the reporter asking my father if he had a car. My father told him, "No, because if I drove, I might get where I am going too fast." That's what he told the reporter. He said that he drives his golf cart to the store and his dog jumps right in it with him.

I loved my father and respected him. I didn't wait until he got sick to tell him I loved him. I would call my father on the phone often to talk to him for hours, and I remember what he used to tell me in our conversations. This stayed with me. He said it only takes a minute to make a mess, then you will be outside with your clothes in your hands, and where you are going, you don't know. I found out how true that was.

*A*s time went on, we had to return to Connecticut. My mother would get together with the family on my father's side and pray before we left. God would always be in our midst with not a dry eye in the house. We would always form a circle, and my mother would pray. A cousin whom I had never seen cry before would break down. My mother would let them know what God was saying. My mother would encourage them.

I remember a couple of months later after we went back home, my cousin called in and said my father was in the hospital, so me, my mother, and my daughters went back to North Carolina. It was his birthday in a couple of days, so we were there with him at the hospital. When visiting him in the hospital, he was in good spirits. Nothing appeared to be wrong. He was up, moving around, talking, laughing, and telling jokes as normal. He wasn't in any pain. He didn't even look like he was sick. My father was a tall, slim man, but he was very strong. He told you exactly what was on his mind without raising his voice as he stood with his arms folded.

I remember my father saying "I ain't going to kill my children, and you save yours."

Oh, boy. It used to make me laugh when I heard him say

that. My father had a lot of sayings. He had a great sense of humor, and I used to love seeing him dance because he could.

As time went on, me, my mother, and my daughters returned home. My father's niece called and said that my father wasn't doing good, so my mother and I went back to North Carolina.

When we reached North Carolina, I went straight to my father's house to see him. The door to his house was open. We walked in, and I went into his bedroom. Then my mother went into the living room. She was praying when we got there. He was in bed in the fetal position, moaning and groaning. I heard him talking to God. He kept on saying, "Help me, God. I am a wretched man. I was praying that you would send somebody."

He was crying. I sat in a chair close to his bedside, praying softly. My father was in excruciating pain. He suffered from unbearable pain in his stomach. I repeatedly said to my mother, "Come pray." I kept prompting her to pray. I recall my mother saying, "I must hear from God first." And she did. She went up in her heavenly tongues and did what God instructed her to do. She came into his bedroom, and so did the Holy Spirit. Readers, I want you to know God showed up in that room right before my very eyes. Also, a mist. There was a breeze that showed up. The room became lighter. I kept hearing, "Listen, listen, listen."

I do believe the Holy Spirit was telling me to listen as my father continued talking to God. Then my father's breathing became lighter and lighter. I saw a miracle. He began to calm down. Then my mother laid her hand on him, and after a while, he got up out of his bed. He started talking to my mother and me. With tears in his eyes, he said, "I asked God to send somebody by here, and he did!"

Then he went outside in his garden. All I could do was thank God for showing up when he did. How he used my mother the way he did, it was a miracle that took place.

I hugged my father. I let him know that I loved him. Then he said, "Susie." That was what he always called me. "If you are going over to town, buy me some face cream." That is what the country folks say in North Carolina to those of you that don't know. I would have brought him anything else he wanted on that day and any other day. I was just so glad that my father was okay.

*M*y mother and I spent a lot of time with him, just talking. She was talking about the goodness of the lord. I remember him saying He may not come when you want Him, but He is always on time. My father always talked about God. I respected him, and I honored him, and I always put something in his hand when I saw him because I read in the bible, Exodus 20:12 KJV, where it says to honor your father and mother that your days might be longer upon the earth.

I remember staying down south for a whole week. Then I had to return home because I had to go back to work. Every time we got together with family, we went out to the country to my aunt and uncle's house where my mother would pray before we left, and I would talk to my cousins. It was kind of strange because a lot of my cousins who I hadn't seen would be there.

It was like whoever was supposed to be there that day was there, and my mother made sure she delivered the word of God to them. Everybody in the house would cry. I even heard one of my cousins giving thanks to God. We always held hands as my mother prayed. We would hug everyone before we left and let them know that we would see them later. Every time we left, my father had a sad look on his face—my aunt, too. They didn't want us to leave. They were happy to see us come and hated to see us go, but we always kept in contact to see how Father was doing.

About a month or so later, my father's niece who always informed us of my father's condition was, called us. This call was not the one I was looking for, readers. My father died. My mother called me and gave me the bad news. So, we had to prepare ourselves once again to go back to North Carolina, and I didn't know if I was ready to see my father stretched out in a casket. It just didn't feel real to me. I thought I was over this part, as far as going to funerals.

Yes, I know we all must die one day, but not my father—not now. When the day came to go to the funeral, me, my mother, brother, and my two daughters went. I was so nervous. My heart was beating so fast. We sat right up in the front row. We were so close to the casket. My father's sister and her husband and brothers, and all my cousins were behind us. There were so many people in that church—a huge crowd of people. People filled the sanctuary to capacity. All the seats were filled. People stood against the wall of the church. It was packed. My father knew a lot of people.

I remember the choir singing. I have cousins who sang in the choir who can really sing, and they are well known for their singing. The pastor was our cousin. He preached at the funeral after the family read the eulogy.

We walked up to view the body. I could hear sobbing. It started. People were going up to the casket to view the body.

I even saw someone taking pictures of my father. I heard someone calling my father's name out loud as they viewed the body.

I looked at my oldest daughter. She started crying, and then my other daughter started crying. I looked down the row at my mother. I truly believe that God had already prepared my mother for my father's death. I never saw her cry. My brother kept repeatedly asking my mother softly, "Are you alright? Is that him?" And then I looked up. My brother had a toothpick in his mouth. He had walked out and then he came back in and took his seat only to ask my mother, "Is it him?" once again.

I remember it was a very hot day. Where was my fan? I was at peace with myself. I always respected my father and did what I could do for him. My father was saved, and I knew one day I would see him again. When it was over, one of our cousins—a sheriff on a motorcycle—escorted the family limousine to the gravesite with the other police officers. People who were walking their dogs stopped. Also, people who were driving stopped to show respect.

After leaving the gravesite, everyone went out to the country to my aunt and uncle's house where they received family and friends. People brought in food—all kinds of stuff—as the day slowly proceeded. We all sat around talking.

*R*eaders, the day of my father's funeral, I couldn't cry as I said my goodbye to him. But the next day when we were driving out to the country, it hit me like a ton of bricks. I couldn't drive. I had to stop and let my daughter drive. All I wanted to do was talk to my father once more like I had done so many times in the past before he got sick. I wanted to see if my father needed anything from the store. I wanted to hug him again and tell him that I loved him no matter what. But he was gone. I kept looking for him to walk through the door at my aunt's house, but he never showed up. That was when I had to realize that my father was gone just like my two sisters. As long as I live, I will never forget the conversations my father and I had. I got to know him. We had a bond. He always gave me good advice. He told me always to keep myself together, no matter what, and don't let anyone mess with me.

And my father had a good heart. He wasn't a hateful or a mean person. He was a very humble man. That is what I saw with every death I have ever experienced. Each one was different. No one is ever prepared for death. It just hits you suddenly, out of nowhere. There was hurt and there was pain in my heart that only God and time could ever heal. I wouldn't wish the kind of pain I experienced on my journey on anyone.

That is why I try so hard to be loving to my family and be kind to everyone I come into contact with—regardless whether they are kind or not—because you don't know when death is going to come and knock on your door. When it does, you will feel it. You will think of all the bad incidents—things you have done to that particular person. And guess what? It's too late to make it right with that person because they cannot hear you anymore. That's the sad part. So you must treat everybody right regardless of whether they like you or not. My view of life? I believe life is like a big Ferris wheel because it keeps on going around and around—every minute, every second, every hour—and as we ride this big Ferris wheel called life, you can rest assured somebody is going to get off this ride. This is accurate every minute, second, hour of every day, week, month, and year. This is reality. I had to understand that no one is here to stay.

*N*ow here on this Ferris wheel called life, somebody's life stopped, so somebody else's life begins. Somebody left, and somebody arrived, and some of them die too quick by being in the wrong place at the wrong time. And then some of them were in the right place and still died young.

There are small graves as well as big graves. I have walked the gravesite looking at various tombstones, and it saddened me, especially when I came across little kids. Now, on this ride with men, women, and children—there is no age limit.

There is someone I heard say this—it comes in threes. Death. I beg to differ. Some people die in groups. Somebody always exits off all the time, and on this ride, there are all kinds of people from all walks of life—even the people you dislike. Also, your enemies—they are on this ride. Your coworkers, your bosses, your next-door neighbors, and your pastors. There are some people on this ride. They are just riding it out, just relaxing as they ride. Do you know why? I will tell you why. These people are relaxing because they are saved. They are the ones who are born again. These are the people who ask God to forgive them of all their sins, so they are safe. But what about you? Because not everyone on this ride is saved. I know it, and they know it. So, as you ride, stop a minute and ask that person on this ride, "Are you saved?" and wait for your answer.

I know we have a choice where we want to end up—heaven or hell. What did you decide? It seems like everyone is having a good time, but that day will come when the master of this ride says, "It's time to stop. This ride is over, and you must get off, and you cannot switch numbers or seats with anyone. Your time is up. The ride stops here."

Prior to me losing my sisters and father, I also lost my uncle back in the day, and my grandfather. I lost a lot of uncles along the way. Some rushed their time away due to alcohol. That took them out of here.

Now, moving forward, my grandmother, who couldn't see any fault in me, loved me unconditionally. She loved me and never judged me. All I kept hearing her say to me was, "One day, God is going to save you, Susan." And I knew she did care and loved me despite my wrongdoings and mishaps. She proved it by opening her doors to me, even when I got kicked out of my mother's house at the age of eighteen.

It was on a Friday afternoon. We were cleaning up. This was when someone brought a big purse with some things in it to my mother's attention. I should not have been in the house in the first place. I was holding something that wasn't even mine. That got me kicked out.

Readers, I always say never mess up where you live. I had messed up tremendously. There was no do-over. I couldn't fix it if I tried. That was it, and I was out. At the time, I didn't know where I was going until I spoke with my grandmother. I wanted to take my daughter, but I knew I couldn't. I was told to leave, so I kissed and hugged my daughter with tears running down my face. Before I left, I called my grandmother who lived close by at the time. I explained a little bit to her on the phone. She said, "Come on over. You can stay with me."

I called the taxi after I talked to my grandmother, so when I reached her house, she offered me some food. Then I began to tell her what had happened. She never judged me. She said, "We are going to pray." My grandmother was a Christian woman. She said, "You are going to be alright because I am going to pray for you." Then she said, "I might not be here to see it, but you are going to be saved." So, I said, "Okay, my mother." That is what all her grandchildren used to call her. We never called her Grandma.

She told me where to put my clothes and where I could sleep. She never questioned me about anything else, and that was fine. I was given a key every morning. My grandmother would be listening to her gospel station and praying for people over the phone. My grandmother did not gossip about anyone. She didn't want to hear other people's gossip or nonsense. What she did want to hear was if you were saved. She was straight to the point.

*I* recall one day some of her other grandchildren had come by to visit her at her new place. She was always glad to see them. Before you could finish your sentence, she said, "Let's pray." So, we all held hands. Before we could start the prayer, one of my uncles called to tell my grandmother something about something. That's when my grandmother didn't want to hear it. She had the phone halfway off her ear. She immediately said to him, "What are you talking about? Isn't worth nothing, boy."

We all fell into laughter. She told her son on the phone, "I have to go. I have company." That was how she said it. It was so funny. We couldn't stop laughing. Then she made sure she prayed. If she found you in a lie, she would say, "You are telling a plum lie." And she didn't allow us to watch television. She would say, "Where in the bible did you see Jesus watched television?" And, "Where in the bible did you see him playing jack rocks?" My siblings, cousins and I used to all fall into laughter.

You couldn't do anything in her house that she didn't approve of but pray and read scriptures, help her set the table for dinner, and run to the store as many times as she asked you. My grandmother would send us to the store over five thousand times if you were visiting her. We made sure we wore comfortable shoes. We knew where we were getting ready to go. If you had a car, that was even better. She didn't care if you were tired of going. You'd better get to getting to that store, and she better not hear you talking underneath your breath. Ouch.

Her favorite two stores back in the day were Kings and Sophie's Corner Store. Cousins, can I get an "amen"? She had her list made out for what she needed at the store, a white handkerchief with her money tied up in it, and she said, "I am sending you to the store. I am giving you this for going to the store. Bring me back my change."

She knew exactly what the items cost, and she knew the owners as well as the managers of these stores. They also knew her in person and by phone because my grandmother shopped at these stores often. My grandmother was a woman who did not play. She walked with character, integrity, and dignity, treated everyone nice, and talked to everybody in the right tone. She set the record straight and always had God in her conversations. The owners at the stores, they showed her respect by using her last name, Mrs. Sykes.

*M*y grandmother would ask so nicely when we left her house. She would say, "Shut my door," with emphasis on it. We all used to laugh about that and still do to this very day. All her grandchildren are still laughing.

She was witty. And when some of the grandkids would do something wrong, she would say, "I am going to take you in that bathroom and peel your behind when you get out of order," and "shut up" when she was talking. It's how she phrased her words that sounded so funny to us. My grandmother had a way with how she used her words. She had a sense of humor, always. She was a sweetheart, a wonderful grandmother—loving, kind, compassionate, generous.

She said, "We are going to pray," and that was what she meant. She most definitely got her prayers though.

She would always prepare breakfast and dinner. She fixed so much food. I thought to myself that some very important people were coming over. She said, "I just like to make sure I have enough in case somebody stops by." Just about every evening, she would cook. If I were around, my grandmother would ask me if I would like some dinner. She would always say, "I am praying for you in the back of my mind." I said to myself, "Oh, I need it."

I always wondered how my daughter was doing—what she was doing. I knew I couldn't go to my mother's house, so I stayed with my grandmother for a little while. She was a Christian woman. She had rules, and I knew them. She would always say to me, "Make sure you close the door when you go out." And when I returned, I had to say who I was, because she had a gun and she would announce that she had one.

So, I stayed at my grandmother's house as long as I could. My grandmother was so loving toward me. I lost my way after the loss of my sisters. I didn't care about anything. All I wanted to do was hang out. I began to think about what I was going to do. I knew I could not live with my grandmother who had welcomed me and still hangout. So, that is when I decided to leave her house. I went to stay with a friend, but she had an animal that I was allergic to, so I thanked her and then I left and went right back to my grandmother's house.

I knew I wasn't going to stay there permanently. I tried to go back to my mother's house by calling to ask if I could come home, but she said no, so I remained at my grandmother's house. I had clothes here, there, and everywhere. I never told anyone my situation until I ran into someone I really thought was a nice person at the time. They kept trying to talk to me. At the time, they helped me get back on my feet. But it wasn't what I truly thought it was, because now this person was abusing me. I kept silent about this.

*A*s you continue reading, you will see as this story unfolds what I am saying. I wasn't truly focused at the time. I just knew I didn't know what steps I was going to take or which way to go. I just knew I had a lot of respect for my grandmother as well as her house. So, I left and got myself into a situation that I didn't see coming because now I was staying here and there—no permanent place to call my own. So I always reached out to certain people for help. I tried to go back home but couldn't. After a period of time, I stopped trying to go back home or reaching out to anyone. But I always thought about my daughter.

I remember one day I ran into someone who asked me how I was doing. I replied by saying, "I am fine."

"Oh," they said to me. "Your mother is looking for you."

I said, "Oh, yeah?"

I couldn't believe it. I was devastated, hurt, confused, and lost for words because I just wanted to ask for forgiveness and move on. That was all I wanted to hear from my mother—"I forgive you."

I wasn't saved at the time. There are no words to describe what I went through. A lot of things occurred. I'll say this: Most of my life I had been distracted by someone or something.

Throughout my life, I had a lot of pluses and a lot of minuses. I have been in the negative as well as the positive. I have fallen and rose out of the ashes so many times. That helped me further know that God has always been with me—the messed up me and the fixed up me. There was no blaming anyone but me, and some things? I brought a lot of things on myself by not listening to the instructor.

Readers, I know one thing: It is so real out there in the world. As I reflect on a lot of events that took place and things that happened to me, I don't ever want to go through it again. I also don't want to remember most of it because it wasn't pretty. I don't ever want to go around hurting people as they hurt me, so when I got by myself, I started to contemplate a lot of things that happened to me. I beat myself up time and time again. I could not believe what had occurred at that point. Yes, I was so wrong in many ways, and I owned it. I also couldn't believe that I got kicked out. It didn't dawn on me until later when I found myself alone and wandering.

That is when it all came into play. That's when I had an eye-opener even though it took a while for me to see the mess I was now facing in my life. This was a lesson learned. I thought that my mother would have mercy on me.

Readers, I didn't know what I was going to do because I was a very young girl. Nothing prepared me for what was out in that world. I was a wild card, I guess, when the situation occurred. She did what she thought she had to do. At that moment, I was very upset by her actions. Of course, at the time, I felt really bad, sad, and ashamed. I know at the time I was not thinking at all.

Now, readers, I must make this very, very clear. Understand this: This is the past, and I love my mother and respect her to the fullest. As time went on, I was able to forgive her. So, when I was asked to remove myself, I encountered a lot of bad habits that were hard to break. I picked up a lot of things along the way and this person who I was trying to avoid for a long time, he was in the picture.

We became friends first, and then he showed me that he could help me, and I didn't have to worry. But I was still worrying, so that was bait. He stepped up, and I stepped up. He started helping me. One day, I said to myself, "I need to have a plan A, plan B, and preferably a plan C."

So, I had met this person, as I shared some time ago, but I would always brush him off. I decided what I was going to do after I left my grandmother's house. I knew I wasn't going to stay with her for a long time out of respect for her, and I had a lot of what-ifs running through my mind.

On that awful day—and readers, I must say this: People do not belong in the street with nowhere to go. Animals belong outside. That is my opinion. Now if you have a dog that you love, keep it in the house. That's frankly up to you because I, myself, love dogs, too. I just prefer they stay in a doghouse. You make the call.

*L*isten closely as you read along. I am not trying to hurt anyone. I assure you of that, as I tell my story of some things that I encountered. Some of the things that happened to me, I will not share because I don't want to go back to that sad, sad place in my life, even though it has passed because it was definitely a sad place at that particular time. But I was told to forgive, so I have because we all must forgive others to move on, and I know forgiveness brings about a change. It wasn't for others, it was all for me—and that is a hard thing to do—forgive. I don't care who you are.

There were a lot of touchy areas in my life that stung me, also a heaviness in my heart—a weight that I couldn't push up for years. I cannot tell you the day, the month, the year, or the time when that weight lifted. I just know it did. It kept trying to cripple me from coming out of that dark place—that cage. Some of you know exactly what I am talking about. I knew if I stayed in that dark place, I wouldn't be here today, but to God be all the glory!

I had to let it go and close the chapter, so I could proceed and move on from that situation, no matter what, and forgive.

Anyway, so for me, I let it go. Yes, I have been hurt so many times to the extreme by so-called people who I thought had my back. I thought they were my friends. I thought they loved me. It's so ironic and disturbing to say that they didn't. It's so funny now. When I look back over my life at what was, the people who hurt me the most wanted me to stay connected to them by sitting down with them, having a hot cup of coffee as well as occupying my space. They, as well as loved ones, weren't exempt.

Yes, I said that. Why lie? And I know readers, we all have had someone in our family who was just not nice at that present time. But guess what? I forgive them, too. You must too, because God? He forgave me so many times and still does because it's in the contract. It was the right thing to do. Now I feel free, not bound. I want my readers to understand where I have been and where I will never return, and the things I experienced on my journey called life. I was in a bad situation, and I didn't have anyone to turn to for moral support when I most needed it. Sometimes the person you do confide in, they don't have a clue themselves. Who could I trust besides my grandmother—the one woman who lived her life without gossiping about other people?

*H*ere I was. I felt alone. Abandoned. Destitute. Broken. I also felt like an outcast. I asked God, "Why did you let me be born?" I was looking. I was searching for something, and I truly didn't know what it was because I was struggling as far as not knowing where I was going to live next after leaving my grandmother's house. I was here and there, clothes everywhere in boxes and bags. I stayed with this person and that person. I was homeless until I reached out to an associate to whom I told my situation. They decided to reach out and try to help me. What next? What could I do when I ran out of options? Well, I would have to go back to my grandmother's house, and I didn't want to do that. I would have to tell her the whole story, not half, so I started to trust this person a little.

He still insisted on helping me, regardless, so I found myself a job and got an apartment. This person was nice. He became an associate. It was too good to be true, readers. So, as time went on, I got back on my feet. I had a roof over my head. So, one day, I decided to go to my mother's house, only because of the conversation that I had with an associate.

So, I went to see my daughter. When I got there, I was told that my daughter was carrying my picture around with her. She was looking for me. Readers, I want to make this clear. When I had my daughter, I didn't give my daughter to my mother. I took care of my daughter. Her father and I were very much a part of her life like he still is today. Yes, my mother raised her. I commend her for that. But regardless of that, she is my daughter. I birthed her into this world, her father and I. Years later we went our separate ways, no grudges on my behalf.

Now, back to my daughter. For the most part, I had my daughter with me until I got kicked out. I made sure I took her to all her doctor's appointments. I used to pick her up and take her shopping. I took her to my apartment on so many occasions. She would stay with me and spend quality time. We also took lots of pictures together. The only place I couldn't take her was the club.

Readers, I want you to understand. It's not about the things I purchased for her at the time. It's about quality time spent with her. I just wanted to say this. Just because you buy your children things, that doesn't make you a good parent. I will never say that I was a bad parent. Life happened to me, and I cannot go back and redo any of it. I can make better decisions moving forward. We do our best. Most children are looking for quality time and love. I don't care who you are, parents are parents. None of us come with a manual. Most of us do what we can do. I repeat, most of us do what we can do.

I did work a lot when I lived with my mother. I was the first girl in the house to have a job. I used to ride my sister's bike to my job early in the morning because I didn't really like relying on anyone. And every Friday when I got paid, I would put my rent money on the table, no questions asked.

I thank God that my mother was able to take care of my daughter, but I always got to see her. I was happy about that. It was the situation I put myself into that robbed me of not raising my daughter the way I truly wanted to. I was absent for a little awhile, but later, after I came around, I stopped being angry with my mother. I began to come around more often.

I was very much present in my daughter's life as much as I could be. I never wanted someone to label me as being a bad parent because we as people love to judge others. Instead of pointing my finger at myself, I did what I could do for my daughter at the time I had her. No, I didn't get the opportunity to raise her the way I wanted to. I thank God for how my mother raised her with good ethics, and I am very proud of that.

Even when she was in school, I attended just about everything she was involved in. I met with teachers and guidance counselors to see how my daughter was doing. I wanted to make sure she graduated and not follow foolishness because when you are in school, you meet all kinds of kids from different walks of life, and there's a group of girls who like you and a group who don't because girls sometimes can be so catty. Why? I don't know.

I love my daughter. I always gave her good advice because I wanted her to grow up and be a powerful woman, be successful, and marry a saved man. That's what I always wanted for both of my daughters.

I will say it again: I always wanted both of my daughters to marry saved men who love them and won't hurt them. What mother doesn't want that for their daughters or sons? I love both of my daughters.

I have always had my daughters' backs, whether they were right or wrong. We can always straighten out the wrong. You best believe that as time went on when I used to pick her up, I would drop her back at my mother's house. Her and her sister, they became very close as they grew up together. They took lots of baby pictures together. I spent time with both of my daughters as much as I could. I just couldn't take them to the clubs because I used to love to party. I always left my daughters with my mother. I wouldn't leave my daughters with anybody else. One of my daughters used to say, "Are you coming back to pick me up?" As I reach down into my purse to give her some candy, I would tell her yes because I didn't want her to be sad. She used to watch me from the window as I drove off into the night.

I always tried to come back before daybreak. Sometimes I would and then sometimes I would pick her up in the morning. When you party in the city, it would be a brand-new day when you came out of the club. So, we would go to the diner afterward and eat breakfast, then go home.

A party could be going on through the weekdays. I went. I loved to party. I loved to hang out with the acquaintances I rolled with. I liked the Jamaicans because they knew how to party and showed you a good time. I was ready. I had a new outfit for every occasion. My associates, acquaintances, and I used to stop at the club's roundabout. It used to have it going on. Then we would end up at another club in another town.

I remember one night, an associate of mine and I were about to leave to go out of town. She said, "Look who is following you."

I looked out my rearview mirror. And behold! To my surprise, I couldn't believe it. There he was right behind me. I hit the gas and drove as fast as I could trying to lose him, only to see him sitting in his automobile at the club I was going to. I told the young lady who I was partying with, "I am not turning around." She kept on asking, "Are you still going in the club?" I told her, "I most certainly am. I came too far to turn around."

Then we both started laughing. Besides, I looked absolutely beautiful, and I wanted to listen to some music to try to free my mind. I don't know what it was about the Jamaican music I listened to, but every time I listened to it, it was so relaxing, and it released the stress that was bottled up in me. So I would get myself a drink, dance, and try to have as much fun as I possibly could. Tomorrow would have to take care of tomorrow. That was how I felt. I wasn't going to let anything or anyone mess up my night, but I knew the next day I would have to face the music, which I will talk about later as my story unfolds.

The associates I hung out with were cool. I will not say their names. They know who they are. But what I *will* say is that I respect each and every one of them. We had lots of fun, and when I tell you *lots of fun*, I mean just that.

We met all kinds of entertainers as well as stars right there in the city. They had it going on and treated us with respect.

*I* remember hanging out one night. I think there were about five or so of us. We were walking in line, all dressed up and waiting to get our hand stamped to go into the club. These guys walking behind us—about five or more—I glanced back at them. They were laughing and joking around. I remember one of them approaching me in the club. I was on the dance floor. He came over to me and said, "You are going to be my woman." I said, "Yeah, right."

As I walked to the ladies' room, that is when he tripped me. I fell into his friend's arms. Then he said, "Oops. Wrong arms," with a smirk on his face and started laughing. I was so embarrassed because there were a lot of partygoers at that club.

Then he started conversing with me, asking where I was from and everything else. I told him where I was from.

I must add this: He was nice looking—good God—tall, slim, and Jamaican. He dressed nice and smelled good. So from that night on, we started hanging out.

Readers, I know what some of you are thinking, "But you have a man!"

No. Not really. To tell you the truth, I was trying to build up enough courage to leave. I already had my plans for getting away from him. I just didn't know when I was going to execute the plan, because how would I do this without being hurt again? How do I get myself out of this situation?

It was already out of control, and this was abuse I'm talking about. This was not a relationship at all. It never felt like it. I was tired mentally. I wanted my life back right away.

That is when he started accusing me of everything. He was so demanding, aggressive, and so verbally and physically abusive toward me. I didn't know it then. The wheels started turning. I knew it was too good to be true. He changed right before my eyes. I was hit numerous times. This was wrong. I was mistreated. This was cruelty. His behavior caused pain. Things were done on purpose. Intentionally, this person was not who I thought.

I remember staying in this room for a while. Reader, it is complicated even to type some parts of this story. Before I got my apartment, he used to come to me, yelling and being very hostile. Then he took a wire hanger and began to unravel it—twisted it around in his hand. I was scared and nervous. I didn't know what this person was up to. Then came a knock at the door.

I ran quickly into the bathroom. I peeked out the door. He left. I locked myself in the bathroom. I was so glad to see him leave. I immediately ran to the door and locked it. That was a scary moment for me. I don't know what he was going to do with that hanger. I didn't know what was running through his mind. I wasn't going to stick around to find out because

I was going to pick up anything that I saw lying around and try my best to knock him out. I just wanted the abuse to stop.

I remember coming in one night. This was when I moved into my apartment. I was hanging out late that night. I saw his truck parked where he always parked it. As I got to the door he put the key in the door. As he entered, the first thing he would ask was, "Where were you last night?" because I drove by.

I never wanted my daughter to see us fight. I kept her away from that because I never knew when he would act out. Most of the time, my daughter wasn't around when I went out to party.

That was the problem. Things appeared to be going fine, but they weren't. When a person is giving you things and starting to take care of you or look out for you, somewhere in the back of their minds, they think that they own you because they are helping you. That's why it's so important to stand on your own feet.

I had my own agenda, and it was to get away from him. When you are hanging out in the street, you kind of know the streets. So basically, I knew the games that people played or tried to play. They had no idea what the price was or what was really going on when they saw me hanging out. You see, they saw the glitz, they saw the glitter, and they saw the glam, but they didn't know what came with it.

*L*et me help you see the picture of what I dealt with. You see, he gave me gifts, and with those gifts came a lot of pretty bows on the boxes. I was so excited to see what was inside those boxes. But you have no idea what's inside of those boxes until you open them up. And that is one box I wish—during that time of my life—that I had never opened.

This predicament that I was in was toxic to my health. So, I say to my readers—please hear me on this—if you know of anyone who is being abused by someone, don't take it lightly. This is serious. It's a cry for help. It could be you or a friend. Please get the help you need. Please hear me on this. Abuse is so serious. It could be deadly. Help before it's too late. You can save a life. Be anonymous about it!

Life is so fun. I have witnessed this a lot in my life. I must say this: Sometimes people are never interested in the person you are with until they see you talking to that person. *Then* they start to get interested.

Wow, and wow.

I have experienced this as well. I say this to make a point— be careful who you bring into your circle, because everything that looks good and smells good may not be good for you. This is real talk. See, at the time, he might have been giving me what I wanted but not what I needed. There is a difference. It was about material things. You cannot put a price tag on peace of mind because I wasn't at peace.

I have heard some women say that things *do* make you happy. I will agree, but only if you get them the right way.

So, every time he got mad, he would act crazy. He would start cursing and screaming—just basically out of control. This was random. It went on for a while, just arguing about everything. The problem was that he really didn't want me to hang out. When I would go out, he got furious. But I was still going out. Besides, I wasn't having it. He was very controlling, and I didn't see the signs—which he hid by appearing to be kind once again.

He appeared to be very kind at first. I was looking to escape all this madness. When he knew he was wrong he would bring me gifts—expensive gifts, all kinds of stuff to make up for the abuse. He would never apologize for what he had done. He would just say, "Huh, do you like these things? Take this." And, of course, I took it. I was so blind and crippled at the time, and I couldn't move if I wanted because the gifts never stopped coming. I was so weak. I tried to remove myself from the situation so many times, but I was afraid and frozen.

Sometimes I would build up enough courage, nerve, and strength, but fear showed up. We all know what happens when fear shows up. It locked me up. I thought he would kill me.

There is a lot I can share in this book and a lot that I cannot. I suffered in silence for many years and never told a soul about the abuse I dealt with.

I remember one night he came over and started again. I heard him coming. He put his key in the door and started shouting, using demeaning words, pushing me, kicking me repeatedly. This was the night I feared for my life because this could have gone in a different direction. I got up and ran through the kitchen. He grabbed a big butcher knife. He tried to pin me against the washing machine. He tried to stab me.

I could see the knife heading for my chest, but I somehow escaped. I ran into the bathroom and locked the door. He kept on being persistent by twisting the doorknob trying to get in but couldn't. I opened the window in the bathroom, jumped down, and ran as fast as I could. It was about two o'clock in the morning, and here I was running for my life. That was one thing I could do was run because I ran track while I was in school.

As I was running I looked back. I saw him coming at full speed. "Oh, God, please help me," I prayed. But he couldn't catch me and I knew it was God because I know for a fact I couldn't outrun that automobile. Even though he was driving, he couldn't catch me. There was a fence up ahead, and I threw my body over it as fast as I could. I thought I had broken my neck and I just laid there on the grass, crying, looking up into the sky, wondering what I was going to do.

I stayed at the park for a little while until I could catch my breath. Then he drove off. After the coast was clear, I went back to the apartment, locked the doors, making sure the coast was clear, and took a shower. I knew he wouldn't return. I knew that the grace of God was with me even in this situation and I know somebody was praying for me, but I continued to be involved with this guy, thinking he would change.

I had put myself in a bad, bad situation and a position that got out of control. I got caught and couldn't get out if I wanted to. And I know some of you readers are asking, "Why didn't you just leave?" Well, it was so hard for me to leave at the time because of fear which had limited me. I was so stuck—like crazy glue—in one spot. And my thoughts were saying to me—and believe me I didn't have enough sense at the time to run away—if my mind was clear enough of all the noise that I let in my head, I could have moved on. I could have made a better decision. At the time I became stagnant because I *could* have thought more clearly—but how could I think clearly when there was *so much fog* around me at the time?

And how could I execute a plan? By saying, "Oh, I'm going to pack up all my stuff. I will leave him tomorrow." I kept on saying it. I was procrastinating every day and couldn't act. When I got to the door, I would look around at the things I had, and my knees would buckle. My nerves were shot. Then I would put all my clothes back in the closet.

Several times I did this. It was like I was in too deep and was too scared to walk away. I remember so many times I should have left, and I know the longer I stayed, the harder it was to hold onto the urge to leave. I couldn't. And if there is some woman out there in a similar situation who's reading my story, she knows exactly what I am saying.

At that time, I was a young girl. I know that things appeared to be going okay, but they weren't at all. I saw things in him that scared me—the anger that built up in him.

I had a jaw-dropping moment. He transitioned so quickly into this other person who I had never met. One day he was nice. The next day I had to cross my fingers. It all depended on what kind of day he was having. I was hoping and thinking things would change, as well as his ways. Then I thought everything would be alright, but how could it be when it was so wrong for me to be involved with him in the first place? I am talking about how he made me feel. Then I would sit and wonder how I got myself into this mess.

I know I should have kept moving the day I ran into him. Readers, guess what? It got worse. I recall one day, sitting and thinking about what might take place that night. I had a plan. I said to myself, "If he comes over tonight acting crazy, it's not going to be good. I will do whatever it takes to defend myself." I had to protect myself. I had to get up a lot of courage and determination. I said, "If I follow through, I guarantee he will never, ever hit me again." So, I got this big rock from behind the house, and I waited for night to fall and for him to act like he was going to put his hands on me.

That night he did, but this time I was ready for whatever. He came into the apartment late at night, crazed out of his mind. That is when he normally showed up. Shouting once again, he grabbed me. He overpowered me like a giant. But I took the rock and grabbed his hair. I kept on hitting him upside his head until my hands got tired. I got strength out of nowhere. I hit him repeatedly. He started walking around while holding his head. Blood was running down his face. I called 911 and spoke with a police officer and told him what had happened. They already knew what was going on because they had a report of domestic violence where I had called them in the past. So, I called the ambulance, and they came to take him to the hospital.

I remember the police officer who knew my family, and he asked me a question. He said, "Why don't you leave him? Do you want us to come back and carry your body out in a body bag?" I told him no. I was afraid, and I couldn't tell the officer everything. I had gotten so comfortable living there. I wasn't thinking at the time. He didn't live with me, but it felt like he did. He paid the rent, so he had the right to a key.

I believed that on the weekends I was being followed. It was like he had someone watching my every move, and he would pay them, and that person would let him know my whereabouts or if I was home or not.

I even took it upon myself to call around town for a support group so I could get out of this situation. I called a women's safe house trying to get away from my abuser. I dialed the number. There was a lady who tried to reassure me that I would be safe. I got scared and froze, so I just hung up and decided not to go. I felt like if I left, he would find me and try to hurt me because of all the stuff he had done for me. Every time I would go out at night, I would be looking over my shoulder to see if I would see him.

I was hoping he would change. I remember getting a job and I stayed in the apartment as though nothing happened for a while. Then things looked like they were getting better, but I started to hang out a lot. And if I *did* go out somewhere, he always had to know my whereabouts. If I came home late and he was at the apartment, he would flip out. One night it was chaos. He came over asking me where I was. I said, "In the city." He assumed I was with someone, and then he hit me with a blow to the head that I didn't see coming. It could have killed me. Blood ran down my face from the gash at the top of my head. I tried to fight back, but he overpowered me. I was dizzy, so I laid helpless on my couch. When he left, I tried to stand up so I could get the medical attention I thought I needed. But I was afraid to go to the hospital because of the incident report that would have been made out and the police would have gotten involved once again. Then he would have probably gone to jail. Then I would have been asked lots of questions pertaining to this incident. So, I avoided it by asking this lady who lived close by with her boyfriend. She was a nice lady. I knocked on her door and asked her to help me. She got some cotton balls and peroxide and began to clean the cut. I asked her if she thought I needed to go to the hospital to get stitches. She said it was okay.

The very next day, a family member came over and rang the doorbell, so I peeked out the window then went to the door. They asked what happened to me because my eye was black and blue due to the object that I was hit with. I don't remember what I shared. I was not going to say anything, so I closed the door quickly. I didn't want anyone to see me in that condition. The very next day, my abuser came around with gifts and money. The only word that came out of his mouth was, "Huh." And that meant, "Here. Take it."

I didn't talk to him for a while. He never apologized. This guy was very possessive, and crazy, and jealous, and unstable at times, which I didn't see until later.

One day we had a bad snowstorm. He came over that night. He said aggressively, "Whose footprints are those outside the door leading from this house?" I explained by saying, "I have no idea what you are talking about." So, I took a look outside because I was in the house the whole day and night due to the storm. Then he said, "I know you had some guy in here," but it was another word he used. I tried to tell him that maybe it was the neighbors who came in, but he kept on. Now, this was the verbal abuse I am talking about. I continued watching television because it takes two to argue, so I ignored him.

If the phone rang, he would pick up the phone trying to say some guy was calling me. So he said, "Don't let me catch you and him." Then he would leave. Then I would breathe easily. But now, every time it snowed—now this is the crazy part—I had to go outside and smooth out the snow and make sure there were no footprints in the snow to avoid confrontation. Just about every time it snowed, I looked out to see if there were footprints or a trail coming from my apartment door so I could go outside and fix it before he came over so he would see there weren't any footprints leading from the house to the walkway. I did this so I could be at peace.

*S*o many times, I feared for my life. I never in my life wished this kind of abuse on anyone. People used to see me all dressed up, out at the clubs, and the first thing some of the ladies would say was, "Oh, you look nice! I like your outfit. I like your hair. I like your shoes." I appeared like I had it all together, so I would say thanks. In the back of my mind, I would say, "If you only knew what I was dealing with behind the mask."

Yes, I said "the mask" because that is exactly what I wore. No, I didn't display any signs of abuse, nor did I confide in anyone—not even the associates I hung with. I was too ashamed of this. This was something I kept hidden for as long as I could. This was very upsetting, difficult, and distressing—as well as embarrassing for me, and complicated to share. This is painful to share. I never wanted to talk about this abuse. Who wants to talk about abuse? No one. But I knew I needed to.

This abuse took me to a very, very dark place in my life. How did I let something like this happen to me? I was never a person to let someone hit me. I know that by exposing myself and being transparent to what I went through, I hope and want to save other women's lives by opening to what I experienced and encountered because I used to be that broken and battered woman.

When I talk about "broken", I mean cracks *everywhere*. My life was shattered. Lots of lost pieces shattered like broken glass all over the place. I was scar tissue—fractured and damaged. I was not together at all. It might have looked like it to others when they saw me because people look at your outer appearance as well as your persona and demeanor, having no clue what is really going on. This weight was heavy on my heart, and I couldn't lift it. I had given up all hope. I took one step and reverted right back. "Hopefully one day," I said, "I will try to escape this abusive man that's in my life."

So, you see, because you can be laughing and crying in the same breath, people didn't realize how messed up I was. Let me explain; Have you ever tried to hide an ugly scar with makeup, only to find out that when the makeup lifts, the scar was still present no matter how well you covered it? It's like trying to remove a bloodstain. The more you rub it, the more that stubborn stain won't move.

It was hard. That was me. I am talking about pain and hurt combined together. I must speak out. I must be vocal about it. I am the voice that women dealing with an abusive man needed to hear. And there are some things I cannot put into context. This wasn't just about outside abuse, because the scars on the outside would eventually heal and vanish. But it was what I was left with that had a grip on me. It really was the after-effects that lingered around me that affected me in so many ways on the inside. It's what I was dealing with mentally as well as emotionally on the inside—my self-worth, my self-esteem, insecurity. I was beaten down, devalued, mishandled. I felt awkward, inadequate, and lacked confidence.

*I*felt battered because I was a battered woman, and no one knew it for years. I didn't tell anyone that anything was wrong because I was too ashamed and afraid. But when I went out, I planned to have a good time by drinking and dancing, trying to escape quietly, even though I didn't know what was in store when I left those clubs.

But I was willing to face whatever. I didn't know what was creeping in the dark or lurking around the corners. Everything looked like it was good, but it wasn't. I was single. I wasn't married to him, but I was married to the things he gave me that I needed to divorce that kept me bound.

I did have a job. It was never hard for me to get a job because I loved to work. So as time went on—I will not say how long—I stayed with this guy. Let's just say, "A day too long that could have cost me my life." This guy was not what I thought. Most of the time, my daughter was at my mother's house. I didn't want her around. This one day, she did witness him hitting me. Then he would stop.

So, when he was out of sight, I called the new guy-friend who I had met. I told him what was going on. I was glad I could talk to him. He was my moral support at the time. He told me that I should leave. That was the advice he gave me. Eventually, I knew I would get up enough courage to leave.

My friend told me several times—he would tell me that I would be okay. He gave me the push that I needed to initiate the plan. He would come to see me just about every single day. He met my family. They liked him. He always wanted to know if I was okay. He asked me one day to show him the guy who I was dealing with. I told him that I was fine. I was just ready to leave town, move on to better things, just start all over, no matter what I had to do—new changes as well as a new life.

He said, "I am moving you out of here." I said, "Where are we going?" He said, "I am moving you out of town." I had already met his family, so he told his mother that he wanted to move out of town. We made arrangements to do so that night.

Before we left, we went to the club. We met up with the associates who I used to hang out with and partied at this club where we had partied so many times before. That night at the party, I told the associates that I would be leaving the next day, so they wished me well. I was so happy to be leaving because I needed a change of scenery. I wanted to be happy again. I wanted my life back. I knew I had to move on with my life and not be so entangled with this guy, so I planned to move away. I had already packed up my stuff along with my daughter's things. I just took our clothes. Everything else I left behind.

I told him I was leaving. He kept trying to convince me and persuade me to stay. I spoke with him over the phone. I believe he told me to keep in touch, but I let him know I couldn't do so anymore. I thanked him for everything he did for my daughter and me. He thought I was playing around. I didn't want anything. I knew I was getting away from him. I didn't care about anything anymore, because, in the back of my mind, I knew he would try to get me back with gifts and promises, trying to sweet-talk me.

While I was dealing with my situation, I found out that my grandmother had been diagnosed with breast cancer. At the time, she lived nearby. I remember one day I visited her, and I kept on smelling something out of the ordinary. I asked my grandmother what that smell was, and she said that it was the garbage. I went to check it out, but I never did see any garbage, so I kind of didn't pay attention to it. I just wanted to see if she was okay.

Some of her other grandchildren would stop by from time to time, and we all smelled the same thing. I knew that awful smell wasn't coming from outside, and everybody who visited would all ask what the smell was. This went on for a while.

I recall my grandmother having a white blanket draped around her shoulder with blood on it, but when I asked about it, she would say, "Oh girl, that is ketchup." So, I wouldn't say anything else about it. But as time went on, one day my brother went to visit her. When he reached her, he found my grandmother stretched out on the floor holding her bible. He called my mother's house to let her know what was going on. I happened to be at my mother's house, so we got in the car and drove to my grandmother's house.

When we got there, my brother and sister said they found

**Susan R Williams**

her on the floor, so my brother called an ambulance, and once they were on the way, my brother said, "Look up under her armpit." What he described to my mother and me was not a pretty sight to see, and I didn't want to see it. I just wanted her to be okay.

So we all gathered around her to let her see that we were there for her—to help her and to give her moral support—so she would take the next step. We basically let her know that she *must* go to the hospital. Some other family members showed up. I didn't want to look at anything as my brother shared what he saw. Then he started telling us that we must get my grandmother to the hospital as soon as possible. So, when the ambulance came, they had a hard time trying to take my grandmother to the hospital because she didn't want to go. She was lying there on the floor in her kitchen with her bible clutched in her hand. We kept on telling her that she had to go to the hospital. She kept on repeatedly saying, "I am *not* going to the hospital! God is going to heal me."

Now a paramedic kept trying to put her on the stretcher, but my grandmother was strong as an ox. She didn't want to go, so everyone kept trying to convince her that she had to go. She finally went, but not quietly. When she got to the hospital, the doctors did tests on her. She was admitted later. They let the family know how long she had breast cancer. That was why there was a smell coming from that hole up under her armpit. She had cancer for ten long years. The doctor diagnosed it.

her on the floor, so my brother called an ambulance, and once they were on the way, my brother said, "Look up under her armpit." What he described to my mother and me was not a pretty sight to see, and I didn't want to see it. I just wanted her to be okay.

So we all gathered around her to let her see that we were there for her—to help her and to give her moral support—so she would take the next step. We basically let her know that she *must* go to the hospital. Some other family members showed up. I didn't want to look at anything as my brother shared what he saw. Then he started telling us that we must get my grandmother to the hospital as soon as possible. So, when the ambulance came, they had a hard time trying to take my grandmother to the hospital because she didn't want to go. She was lying there on the floor in her kitchen with her bible clutched in her hand. We kept on telling her that she had to go to the hospital. She kept on repeatedly saying, "I am *not* going to the hospital! God is going to heal me."

Now a paramedic kept trying to put her on the stretcher, but my grandmother was strong as an ox. She didn't want to go, so everyone kept trying to convince her that she had to go. She finally went, but not quietly. When she got to the hospital, the doctors did tests on her. She was admitted later. They let the family know how long she had breast cancer. That was why there was a smell coming from that hole up under her armpit. She had cancer for ten long years. The doctor diagnosed it.

He also said she must have known a higher power. They were amazed that she lived that long.

I remember her having bad headaches. She would call my mother and ask her to pray. Later, my grandmother was transferred to a nursing facility where she was taken care of. Family and friends would visit her periodically to see how she was doing. She was always in good spirits and always prayed. She enjoyed company. She never appeared to be in any kind of pain. When I went to visit her, I told her that I loved her like I always did.

So, I went on with my plans. I moved away with my friend and daughter. I would always call and ask how my grandmother was doing. My mother would say she was fine until that sad day I received a call that I did not want to receive from my mother saying that my grandmother had died.

Everything started coming back to me—my two sisters, my father, and now my grandmother. I told my friend that I had to go back home to see my grandmother. I had a special bond with my grandmother. I did love my grandfather, as well, who had a sense of humor. He used to make me laugh. He used to say, "I am honey, but the bees don't know it!" I wasn't as close to my grandfather as I was to my grandmother. My oldest sister was.

Moving on, we prepared to leave the next day, so my friend called a close friend of his and asked him to drive us to Connecticut. I couldn't stop crying. I remember all the conversations that we shared, the things she told me, how she treated me, how she loved me, how she nurtured me. Nobody could tell me that my grandmother didn't love me. She didn't just say that word. She proved it over and over again. I always saw the love of God in her.

She wouldn't let anybody talk about me. She would always come to my defense. She would check them right where they stood and say, "Oh, not Susan. Oh, no, no."

She told me one day that I would be saved as she continued to pray for me. And readers, when I talk about my grandmother, I can go on and on. That's how special she was to me. I heard her tell some of the family members one day, "Oh, no. Susan isn't going to tell me no lie. If she said she is coming, she is coming." And I would be right there. I always visited my grandmother, making sure she was okay. She would have her bible open on her table, or she would be on the phone praying for others. I would always ask my grandmother if she needed me to do anything while I was there, or perhaps go to the store. I would hug her and tell her that I loved her. She was glad to see me.

As always, my grandmother kept repeating this as she looked at me: "You are going to be saved, so you might as well get ready." I never lied to her about anything because she basically already knew if you were lying or telling the truth. I knew all the while that my grandmother was praying for me. So many times, when I felt like nobody loved me, she did.

*S*o, back to Connecticut.

When we reached Connecticut, we went to my mother's house. My aunts and family were there. I had cried so much that my eyes were swollen. My aunt thought my friend had beaten me up. That wasn't the case at all. This guy was not like that at all.

The day of my grandmother's funeral, I stood up to say a couple of words. I couldn't believe she was gone. I said my goodbye to her, and I knew one day, when I got myself together, I would see her again after everything was over. I spent a little time with my other daughter and my mother, then me, my daughter, my friend, and his best friend who drove us, said goodbye to my family and headed back home.

On the way back, my friend kept asking me if I was okay. I told him that I would be. When we got home, I stayed down there for some months, then I wanted to return to Connecticut. I started to feel very sad and depressed. I missed my daughter, and because of my grandmother's death, I wasn't the same person.

Readers, hold on. I got in contact with the guy I left. I told him that I would be returning. Then he said to let him know, and he would get me a rental to bring all my stuff back to Connecticut.

On the day of my arrival back to Connecticut, one of my sisters was having a baby shower, so I immediately went to my mother's house where the baby shower was being held and stayed there. I was so glad to see my other daughter as well as my other family members.

I had a conversation with my friend before I moved back, so he was fine with it. He went back to his mother's house, and I went back to Connecticut to stay, only to see the guy I left who wanted to talk to me on my arrival. He told me that the apartment was still available, and everything was the way I left it.

Readers, okay, I know what some of you are saying. When I left Connecticut, we kept in contact. I know this sounds crazy, but I believe anybody can change if they want to. At least, I thought so. We met up and hooked up again, and then we began to talk about a lot of things. I told him I wanted to be closer so I could see my daughter, then he gave me a key to the apartment so that I could put my stuff in it. When I went to my apartment, everything was nice and clean like the way I had left it. He also shared with me that he asked someone he knew to come over to the apartment from time to time and dust.

In the back of my mind, I remember what my friend said who told me I should not go back, but I was kind of homesick. I wanted to see my daughter. I was not thinking straight after losing my grandmother. I wanted to be close to home in case something else happened, and I wanted to see my family.

So, as time went by, my friend from the city and I, we still saw each other. We kept in touch periodically. When I settled back into my apartment, things were going well for a while. I got the key back to my apartment and found a job. I didn't want this guy in my life anymore. I knew what I was doing, so sometimes I would try to stay close to home because I didn't want any problems. I would tell my friend where to pick me up, or he met me at the club.

I continued to hang out with my friends in the city where the nice clubs were. My friend was very well known. He was like a V.I P. at a lot of clubs, and at some, he knew the owner. I remember one night my friend came by my mother's house. My father was there at the time. He was talking to me. He had so many plans—things he wanted to do, places he wanted to go that he wanted to take me. He was planning for him and some friends of his to have a big fashion show with some of the well-known models out of town. He wanted them to come to Connecticut.

So, he asked me if I was going out that night, and I told him no, that I was staying home. That evening, I saw him. I talked to him briefly. I told him to go home and tomorrow I would go see him. He was sitting at the table that evening. He kept rubbing his head. He said, "Sue-sue,"—that is what he called me—"One day I am going to take you someplace you never been." I said I would love to go, and then he told me he was going home. I said okay and I hugged him. Then he left. Then an associate of mine had car trouble, so I had to go pick her up, and I brought her back to her house.

After I dropped her off I went to my mother's house to pick up my daughter, and after that I went home and couldn't sleep the whole night. I kept feeling kind of weird. I couldn't shake it off. But I recalled my sister saying something that same night. I didn't pay any attention to what she was saying. She felt like somebody was going to die that night.

At about three or four in the morning, the doorbell rang. This girl came by with some bad news. I was wondering what was going on. She was crying. I thought she had a fight with someone, so I asked her what happened. That was when she said, "Your friend got shot."

I couldn't think. I was in a state of shock. I kept on asking who. Then she said his name. I asked where he was because I wanted to see him. She said he was at the hospital, so I woke up my daughter, got her dressed, and then I went to the hospital. When we got there, I saw this nurse who was on duty. I told her my friend's name. She asked who I was, and I told her that I was his fiancé so I could see him. That is when she told me to come with her. We walk into an empty room. That was when she told me that my fiancé had expired. That was when I passed out. When I regained consciousness, the person who came with the bad news told me that everything would be all right. My daughter was just looking at me. She was too young to understand what was going on.

When I left the hospital, I went to my apartment and called his mother, who had already received the bad news. Then I got myself dressed, and an associate of mine and I went to the city. When I got there, his family wanted answers. I couldn't explain anything because I truly did not know what had happened.

I was very hurt and sad. I was grieving like everybody else. I had lots of flashbacks of us together. We were everywhere. We went on a lot of boat rides, parties. For the most part, he treated me very nice. He'd had my back no matter what, and I also had his back.

My friend's mother always treated me like family. Sometimes, when we went out to the club, she would ask me if I was going to stay the night because it was late. When I *did* stay, she would put each of us in separate rooms. She let everyone who was at her house know that her son loved me, and she knew it.

The family wanted answers, and I had no answers because I truly didn't know what had occurred. I had nothing to share, so I hugged his family to let them know that I was so sorry for their loss. I felt so sad myself, and I was hurt and disappointed. So, I gave my sympathy. I was looking for answers myself and I kept in touch with the family.

I kept going to pay my respects to the family because his mother was like a mother to me. She always welcomed me with open arms and never treated me any other way. I went to my friend's funeral to say goodbye to him, and after everything had settled down, I continued to keep in touch.

I told his mother that I would always remember the good times we had together. We went to a lot of places. One year, I even invited him to have Thanksgiving dinner with my family. My family liked him as well, and we spent a lot of time together. We took plenty of pictures as well, and I met a lot of his family. They treated me so nice. He loved my daughter. He used to always pick her up and carry her on his back.

He used to tell me, "I love you bad, bad, bad!" That used to make me laugh. He even bought me these big, gold earrings from back in the day that had Sue-Sue engraved on each one of them. How I loved those earrings!

*A*s time went on, I kind of wondered if we would have gotten married because he didn't just tell me he cared about me, he showed me. We shared some precious times together just by him being there when I needed someone the most.

I kept saying, "What if I had stayed? Would he still be here?"

I remember, one day I was in my bed—true story, readers—he came to me. He had on all white. He was smiling and he looked nice. He said, "Boo! Look at you. You are scared!" And I was, readers.

As I look back on our time together, I remember one day; I was in the city going to visit him with my daughter because he wanted to go see an associate of his to plan a party. I picked him up at his mother's house. I asked my daughter if she wanted to stay with my friend's mother. She wanted to go with me, so we went to meet with the owner of this club to prepare for the party.

I took my daughter with us to the club. This was in the daytime. I didn't see any harm in it because when I got dressed to go out, she would say, "Mom, where are you going?" and I would say, "To the club out in the city." She was five years old at the time, but she was so curious, so I took her in to see where I was partying. My friend started talking to the owner, so they talked for a while and then we left to go to his mother's house.

I put my daughter in the car and put on her seatbelt. As we were riding, we were playing music and talking, and suddenly I looked back and I did not see my daughter. I started screaming. The door of my car was open. That is when I heard this lady screaming. She was saying, "Your daughter! Your daughter!"

My friend backed the car up, and there was my daughter lying by the side of the road where the buses stop. She was crying, so my friend picked her up quickly and put her in the car. We rushed to his house. I sat in the back seat with her, just looking at her face. Her face appeared to be fine, but she had minor scrapes.

I was nervous because this situation could have gone another way. I knew God had his angels watching over my daughter. I was so scared and shaking. I did not take her to the hospital in the city. I took her straight to his mother's house because I knew that his mother had some type of home remedy that she could put on the scrapes and bruises that I saw on my daughter's knees and elbow. I trusted her, so when we got to the house, we brought her into his mother's bedroom. She started yelling, "What happened? What happened to the pickney?" In Jamaican language, "pickney" means "kid". So, we tried to explain things to his mother. She was so furious at us. I felt like she wanted to beat both of us. My friend kept walking back in fourth, rubbing his head. That was a sign to me that he was also nervous. His mother took my daughter. She washed her up and put some brown medicine on her elbow and knees, and then put her in the bed with her. I think she told us to get out and leave the pickney with her.

That was one of the scariest days of my life. My friend and I kept talking about it. My daughter, she could have gotten killed! I was hysterical. I truly thanked God for sparing my daughter's life on that day, and before I left, I thanked his mother for what she did when I left the city.

I took my daughter to the hospital when I got home, they checked her out, and she had no broken bones. I was so grateful to God once again. I shared what had happened with my family. Everyone knew it was a miracle. My daughter was fine. When I heard my daughter cry on that day, that was a good sign that she was alive, and I know for a fact that God had his angels around her because there was a lot of traffic coming down that day. I know that God had his angels to scoop my daughter up that day and let her know she was safe in his arms. Hallelujah, hallelujah. I know this was a miracle. Thank you, God.

I couldn't stop hugging and kissing my daughter, because this story could have definitely read another way, and as long as I live I will never forget what God did for my daughter on that day.

So, readers, as you continue following me on my journey,

you will see the things I endured, the pain that I tried to hide, and the tears that I have cried.

Yours truly,
*Susan R. Williams*

Printed in the United States
By Bookmasters